THE EMPEROR PENGUIN

Written by Sally Grindley
Illustrated by Mandy Doyle

Collins Educational
An Imprint of HarperCollins*Publishers*

This is the land of snow and ice. This is the land where even in summer the ice does not melt. This is the land where there are no trees and no flowers and no butterflies and no bees.

This is the land where the Emperor Penguins live.

It is the middle of winter, when the sun never shines and the night lasts all day. This Emperor Penguin has been standing still for sixty-three days. He has not moved.

Even when the icy wind blows around him, he does not move. He must not move.

On his feet there rests an egg. The loose skin on his belly covers it and helps to keep it warm. The Emperor Penguin's mate has given him their egg to look after while she is away on the long search for food.

One day the Emperor Penguin will be a father, if he looks after the egg well.

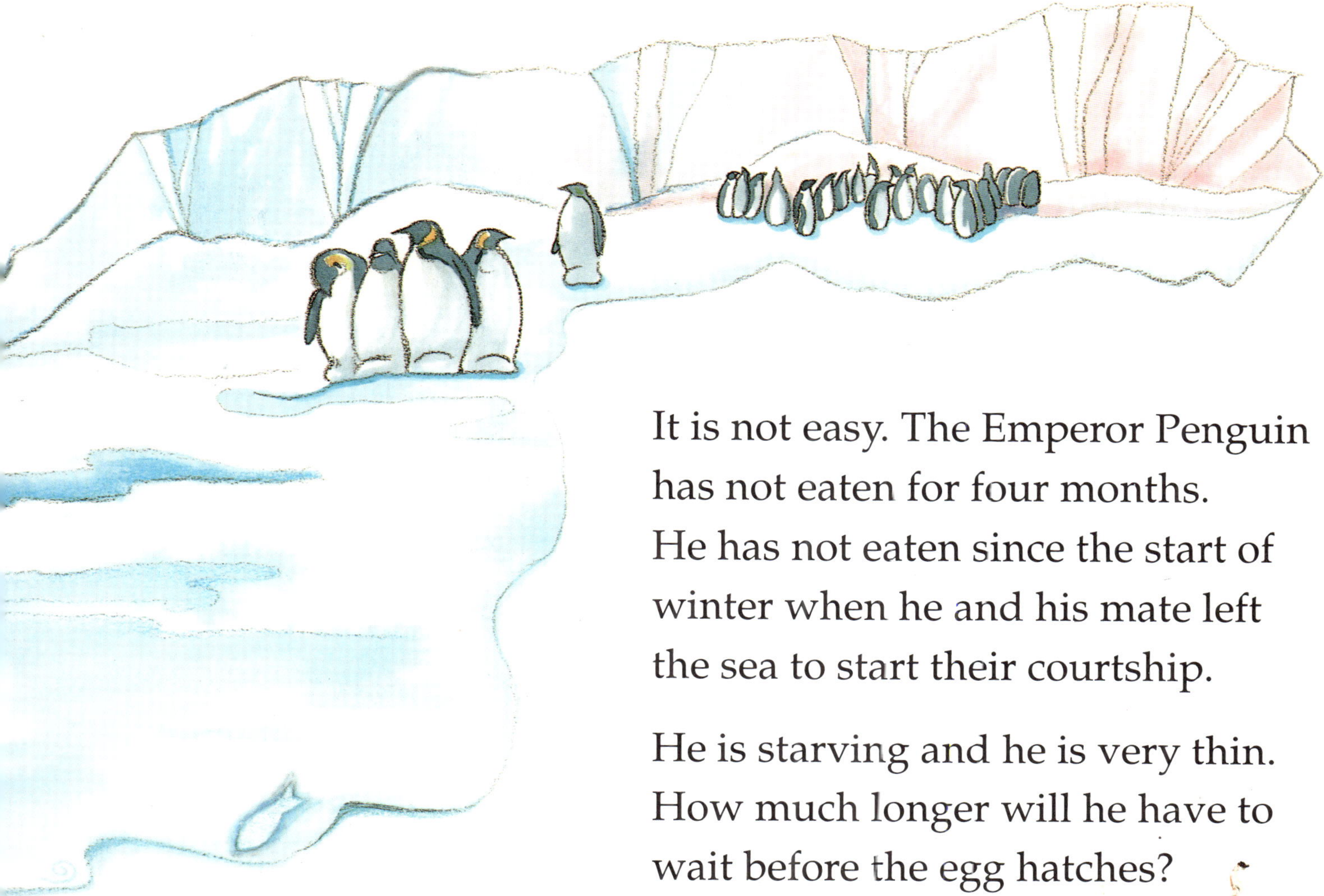

It is not easy. The Emperor Penguin has not eaten for four months. He has not eaten since the start of winter when he and his mate left the sea to start their courtship.

He is starving and he is very thin. How much longer will he have to wait before the egg hatches?

The Emperor Penguin is not alone. He huddles together with dozens of other male penguins. They, too, are keeping their eggs warm. They, too, are starving thin. Together they wait anxiously until their chicks are hatched and their mates return.

The moment they have been waiting for arrives. The Emperor Penguin feels a tap-tap-tapping on his feet. He feels the egg cracking. He feels something soft and tiny moving about.

He looks down and sees his chick still wrapped in the fold of his belly. As hungry as he is, he knows he must feed his tiny male chick.

From deep in his stomach, he manages to find enough food to pass into his chick's open mouth. The Emperor Penguin looks around. Many fathers are feeding their newborn chicks with their very first meal. And then, across the icy wastes, he sees the female penguins returning.

While the Emperor Penguin has been caring for their egg, his mate has travelled many miles. She has walked and tobogganed across frozen seas to reach warmer waters. There she has fattened herself up on fish, ready for the day when she must return to feed her chick.

The Emperor Penguin waits anxiously for his mate to call. Has she come back with the others? He knows that if she does not come back, their chick will die. He cannot feed it. He has no more food to give.

Then he hears her and he calls in reply. The Emperor Penguin's mate knows his call. She waddles over to him and sees her new chick for the first time.

She knows what to do. She must feed her chick straight away. She bends down and carefully passes food from her stomach into the little chick's begging mouth.

The Emperor Penguin's mate must now look after their chick. The chick moves over onto its mother's feet.

The Emperor Penguin is free at last to go and find food for himself. He joins the other male penguins, who walk and toboggan across the miles of frozen sea until they reach the warmer waters.

For two weeks, the Emperor Penguin swims and dives and gorges himself on fish. He needs this rest to recover from the hard winter. Then he makes the long journey back to his mate, and their chick, with a stomach and a crop full of fish.

The chick eats hungrily. He is growing fast and needs food to build up his strength. He is too big now to sit on his parents' feet. He spends his time huddled together with all the other chicks to keep out the cold.

The Emperor Penguin and his mate take it in turns to go fishing and bring back food for the hungry chick.

But winter is nearly over.

As the days grow lighter and warmer, cracks begin to appear in the frozen ice. It will soon be time for the chick to feed himself. Soon the ice cracks right by the chicks' nursery. The water shines brilliant blue and icy cold.

The chicks shuffle down to the edge and dive in. They are excellent swimmers.

The Emperor Penguin and his mate, and all the other adult penguins, join their chicks in their fishy feast. For two months they gorge themselves.

The Emperor Penguin's chick has now lost his fluffy brown feathers. His feathers are thick and shiny like his father's. He has grown fit and fat and can keep himself warm.

Winter is fast approaching. The long, dark days will soon begin. The penguins leave the water and move back to their breeding grounds. In a short time the seas will be frozen over again.

In two or three years' time, the Emperor Penguin's chick will be ready to find a mate. He will begin his courtship, and for two months he will display to the female penguin of his choice.

When they have mated, she will lay their egg. As soon as she does, she will lift it onto her feet, shuffle over to him and place it carefully on his feet.

After sixty-four days, the Emperor Penguin's chick will be a father, if he looks after the egg well.